Food for Life

MOUNTAINS

KATE RIGGS

Published by Creative Education
P.O. Box 227, Mankato, Minnesota 56002
Creative Education is an imprint of The Creative Company
www.thecreativecompany.us

Design and production by Liddy Walseth
Art direction by Rita Marshall
Printed in the United States of America

Photographs by Alamy (blickwinkel), Corbis (Charles Krebs), Getty Images
(Altrendo Nature, China Photos, Jim and Jamie Dutcher, Tim Fitzharris,
Melody Ko, Steve Lewis, John E. Marriott, David McNew, Tom Murphy,
David Ponton, Ron and Patty Thomas, Tom Tietz, Joseph Van Os, Ian Waldie)

Library of Congress Cataloging-in-Publication Data
Riggs, Kate.
Mountains / by Kate Riggs.
p. cm. — (Food for life)
Includes index.
Summary: A fundamental look at a common food chain in the mountains,
starting with the ponderosa pine, ending with the mountain lion, and
introducing various animals in between.
ISBN 978-1-58341-827-7
1. Mountain ecology—Juvenile literature. 2. Food chains (Ecology)—
Juvenile literature.
I. Title. II. Series.

QH541.5.M65R555 2010
577.5'316—dc22 2009004780

First Edition
2 4 6 8 9 7 5 3 1

Food for Life

MOUNTAINS

KATE RIGGS

A GREEN BOOK

A food chain shows what living things in an area eat. Plants are the first link on a food chain. Animals that eat plants or other animals make up the rest of the links.

Mountains are tall, rocky hills. They can be found all over the world. Some mountains have forests with lots of trees. Some mountains have snow covering them year-round.

GOLDEN EAGLES USE
TO FIND *RODENTS*,

THEIR GOOD EYESIGHT
RABBITS, AND BIRDS TO EAT.

Pine trees grow on some mountains. They are evergreen trees. They have green needles instead of leaves. The needles never change color like leaves do. Some animals eat seeds from pine trees.

Pine beetles like to eat another part of the pine tree. They eat the bark. Pine beetles have mouths that move like a pair of scissors. It is easy for them to chew through the bark.

SNOW LEOPARDS LIVE ON COLD MOUNTAINS ON THE _CONTINENT_ OF ASIA. THEY EAT LARGE SHEEP.

Woodpeckers use their strong beaks to peck through tree bark. **But they do not eat the bark.** They eat the pine beetles. A woodpecker can eat thousands of beetles a year!

THE ANDEAN (AN-dee-en)
SCAVENGER. IT EATS THE

CONDOR IS A MOUNTAIN
LEFTOVERS OF DEAD ANIMALS.

Martens also live in pine trees. They are related to weasels. Martens eat woodpeckers. They look for woodpecker nests and eat the eggs or young birds.

Martens are like snacks for hungry mountain lions. The large cats quietly sneak up on the small martens. Then they jump to attack their _prey_.

GIANT PANDAS LIVE IN
THEIR MAIN FOOD IS A

THE MOUNTAINS OF CHINA.
PLANT CALLED BAMBOO.

All of these living things make up a food chain. The pine tree grows on the side of the mountain. The pine beetle eats the bark of the tree. The woodpecker eats the beetle. The marten eats the woodpecker. And the mountain lion eats the marten.

THE PLANT-EATING PIKA
IS RELATED TO RABBITS.
IT IS HUNTED BY GOLDEN
EAGLES AND MARTENS.

Some day, the mountain lion will die. Its body will break down into _nutrients_ (NOO-tree-ents). These nutrients will go into the ground and help plants such as the pine tree grow. Then the mountain food chain will start all over again.

READ MORE ABOUT IT

Galko, Francine. *Mountain Animals*. Chicago: Heinemann Library, 2003.
Spilsbury, Louise, and Richard Spilsbury. *Mountain Food Chains*. Chicago: Heinemann Library, 2005.

GLOSSARY

continent—one of Earth's seven large pieces of land

nutrients—things in soil and food that help plants and animals grow strong and healthy

prey—an animal that is killed and eaten by another animal

rodents—animals such as rats, mice, or squirrels that have strong front teeth

INDEX